GOD'S CREATURES
IN THE WOODS

GOD'S CREATURES
IN THE WOODS
Mothers and Their Babies

by
Debra K. Stuckey

Illustrated by
Jules Edler

Publishing House
St. Louis

Copyright © 1986 Concordia Publishing House
3558 S. Jefferson Avenue, St. Louis, MO 63118-3968
Manufactured in the United States of America

All rights reserved. No part of this publication may be reproduced, stored in a retrieval system, or transmitted, in any form or by any means, electronic, mechanical, photocopying, recording, or otherwise, without the prior written permission of Concordia Publishing House.

Library of Congress Cataloging-in-Publication Data
Stuckey, Debra K., 1959-
  God's creatures in the woods.
  Summary: Demonstrates how God cares for His woodland creatures by giving them parents to look after them.
  1. Forest fauna—Religious aspects—Christianity—Religious aspects. 2. Creation—Juvenile literature. [1. Parental behavior in animals. 2. Forest animals—Infancy] I. Edler, Jules, ill. II. Title.
BT746.S78   1986   215′.74   85-17088
ISBN 0-570-04135-X

1 2 3 4 5 6 7 8 9 10 PP 95 94 93 92 91 90 89 88 87 86

**To
Rachel and Joshua**

God cares for His creatures in the woods. The young ones need help, so God gave them parents to care for them until they're grown. Isn't God wise?

"Quack, quack," calls
Mrs. Duck.
Her ducklings follow her
in a long line.
This is God's way to
keep them safe.

Mother Robin finds a fat worm for her babies.
God makes them grow so they can learn to fly.
Watch them go!

God gave Mrs. Oppossum a special warm pouch.
She carries her tiny babies there.
When they grow bigger, they ride on her back.

I wish I could play with the cute, spotted fawn.
But his parents know better.
God gave them
strong legs and taught them to run from danger.

No one will harm the skunks' babies.
God gave them smelly spray for protection.
Phew! Let's not get too close.

**Raccoons teach their babies to find berries and bugs and wash them. They sure think berries and bugs are tasty.
I'm glad God gives me other food.**

Mother Bear shows her cubs how to find honey. The bees can't sting the cubs through the thick fur God gave them. Honey—what a yummy meal!

Squirrels teach their young
ones to jump
from limb to limb. What fun!
God made it hard for others to
catch them.

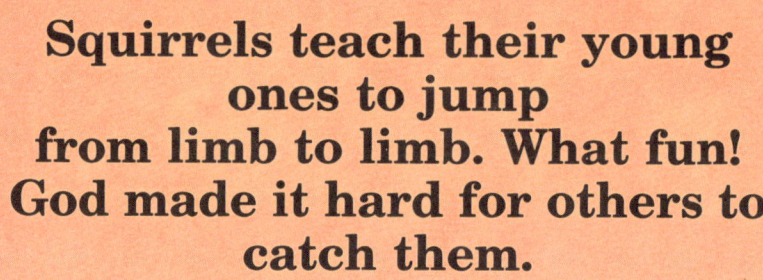

**God gave me parents, too.
He knows how much
I need them
to teach me and care for me.**